OLYMPIC
SPORTS

Great Moments in
Olympic
ICE HOCKEY

By Chris Peters

SportsZone

An Imprint of Abdo Publishing
www.abdopublishing.com

www.abdopublishing.com

Published by Abdo Publishing, a division of ABDO, PO Box 398166, Minneapolis, Minnesota 55439. Copyright © 2015 by Abdo Consulting Group, Inc. International copyrights reserved in all countries. No part of this book may be reproduced in any form without written permission from the publisher. SportsZone™ is a trademark and logo of Abdo Publishing.

Printed in the United States of America, North Mankato, Minnesota
042014
092014

THIS BOOK CONTAINS
RECYCLED MATERIALS

Cover Photo: Chris O'Meara/AP Images
Interior Photos: Chris O'Meara/AP Images, 1, 48; AP Images, 6–7, 10, 14–15, 17, 21; Bettmann/Corbis, 13; Wally McNamee/Corbis, 22–23; Denis Paquin/AP Images, 25, 37; Paul Chiasson/AP Images, 29, 43; Hans Deryk/AP Images, 30–31; Kevork Djansezian/AP Images, 33; Lawrence Jackson/AP Images, 38–39; The Canadian Press/Tom Hanson/AP Images, 45; Gene J. Puskar/AP Images, 46–47; The Canadian Press/Jonathan Hayward/AP Images, 53; Matt Slocum/AP Images, 54–55, 59

Editor: Chrös McDougall
Series Designer: Craig Hinton

Library of Congress Control Number: 2014932860

Cataloging-in-Publication Data
Peters, Chris.
 Great moments in Olympic ice hockey / Chris Peters.
  p. cm. -- (Great moments in Olympic sports)
Includes bibliographical references and index.
ISBN 978-1-62403-395-7
1. Hockey--Juvenile literature. 2. Winter Olympics--Juvenile literature. I. Title.
796.9--dc23

2014932860

Contents

Introduction 4

1 Lake Placid 1980:
Miracle on Ice 7

2 Squaw Valley 1960:
The Forgotten Miracle 15

3 Nagano 1998: The NHL Arrives 23

4 Nagano 1998:
The Women Debut 31

5 Salt Lake City 2002:
Canada's Time 39

6 Vancouver 2010:
Sid the Kid Delivers 47

7 Sochi 2014: Next-Level Rivals 55

Great Olympians   60
Glossary   61
For More information   62
Index   64
About the Author   64

Introduction

Ice hockey's origins have been debated for decades. Canadian James Creighton is credited with helping organize the first official hockey game in 1875 in Montreal, Canada. The sport made its Olympic debut at the 1920 Summer Games in Antwerp, Belgium. Canada took the gold medal, with Team USA taking the silver.

Four years later, the first Olympic Winter Games were held in Chamonix, France. Hockey has been a part of every Winter Olympics since. The Winter Games were held the same year as the Summer

Games until 1992. Since 1994, the Winter and Summer Olympics have been separated by two years.

The 1998 Olympics were the first in which National Hockey League (NHL) players were allowed to play. It was also the first year that women's hockey became part of the Olympics.

Through 2014, Canada leads the all-time gold-medal count with nine in men's hockey, including three in the NHL era, and four in women's hockey. The Soviet Union won seven gold medals in men's hockey and claimed another as "The Unified Team" in 1992 after the Soviet Union dissolved. The United States has two gold medals and eight silvers in men's hockey and one gold and three silver medals in women's hockey.

1

Lake Placid 1980
MIRACLE ON ICE

The famous call began. "The countdown going on right now . . . Morrow up to Silk . . . Five seconds left in the game . . . Do you believe in Miracles? YES!"

Those were the words of legendary broadcaster Al Michaels as he called the closing seconds of the game that became known as the Miracle on Ice. The US Olympic hockey team beat the mighty Soviet Union 4-3 in the medal round of the 1980 Olympic Winter Games in Lake Placid, New York. Many believe it is the greatest upset in sports history.

Team USA celebrates after beating the Soviet Union at the 1980 Olympic Winter Games in Lake Placid, New York.

Team USA coach Herb Brooks knew he could field a team that could compete. But no one expected the US squad to win a gold medal. After all, the Americans were all amateurs and college players. The Soviets, meanwhile, were the best in their country and supported by the government. Even US captain Mike Eruzione said before the tournament that most people would pick his team to finish fifth.

Meanwhile, the United States was a struggling country. Many people were out of work. There was a shortage in gasoline for Americans to run their cars. The Cold War between the United States and the Soviet Union was still a source of great worry. Just a few months before the Olympics, more than 60 Americans were taken hostage in the US Embassy in Iran.

Then Brooks and his 20 scrappy college kids came along. Brooks and his team weren't trying to solve the United States' political problems. But they could try to be a distraction.

Bill Baker Saves USA vs. Sweden

The Miracle on Ice might never have happened if not for a wild Team USA comeback in the first game of the 1980 Olympics. The Americans trailed Sweden 2–1 with only 41 seconds left. US coach Herb Brooks pulled goalie Jim Craig for an extra attacker. Defenseman Bill Baker, a standout at the University of Minnesota, drove a hard shot to the net and past Sweden's goalie. The game ended 2–2. Team USA got a much-needed point and a lot of confidence.

Brooks also knew his squad would have a tough schedule in Lake Placid. It would have to play the likes of Sweden and Czechoslovakia in the preliminary round. Both of those teams presented Team USA with quite a challenge. The Americans pulled off a big surprise, though. They made it through the first round with four wins, no losses, and a tie.

The Medal Round

Team USA was one of four teams that qualified for the medal round. It was not a single-elimination format like today. Instead, the top two teams from each preliminary group played the top two teams from the other group. For Team USA, that meant games against the Soviet Union and Finland.

Known as "The Big Red Machine," the Soviet hockey team had won the gold medal at the previous four Olympics. And the Soviets beat Team USA 10–3 in a pre-Olympic exhibition. But the US players went into the game knowing they had an unforgettable opportunity in front of them. If they played as a team, they believed they had a chance.

Then the Soviets scored the first goal of the game. It looked like Team USA was in for another beating. That was until Buzz Schneider stepped up. Schneider was Team USA's oldest player at 25 years old. He took the puck and streaked into the Soviet zone, then fired a hard slap

Tensions were high going into the 1980 Olympic medal-round hockey game between Team USA and the Soviet Union.

shot at the net. The puck soared over the outstretched glove of goalie Vladislav Tretiak.

The Soviet Union scored once again, though, to make it 2–1. The first period was coming to an end. It was looking like Team USA would head into the locker room trailing. Then, with five seconds remaining, the Americans had an amazing run of plays.

Dave Christian, the son of an Olympic gold medalist, sent a shot from center ice at Tretiak. The Soviet goaltender kicked it away easily. But with barely any time left, the puck ended up on Mark Johnson's stick. The speedy forward from the University of Wisconsin calmly collected the puck and made a move on Tretiak. As the puck crossed the goal line, the buzzer sounded. The goal counted. The game was tied 2–2.

Soviet coach Viktor Tikhonov decided that Tretiak should be taken out of the game. Backup goalie Vladimir Myshkin was sent in to take his place. Many in hockey believed Tretiak to be the best goalie in the world. And now he was sitting on the bench.

Back and Forth

The second period belonged to the Soviets. They kept shots coming on US goaltender Jim Craig. One of those shots went in to make it 3–2. Team USA went into the third period down one goal.

But the Americans came out flying to start the third period. They knew they were close enough to mount a comeback. That's when Johnson played hero again. Dave Silk's pass made it through a couple of Soviet defenders and settled onto Johnson's stick. He slipped it past Myshkin to make it 3–3.

That set the stage for one of the most famous goals ever scored in hockey. The third period neared the halfway point. Eruzione grabbed a loose puck just inside the Soviet blue line. As Eruzione picked up his head, he saw a lane to shoot through. Eruzione swept his stick back and fired a hard wrist shot. Myshkin couldn't get his pads out in time to stop the low shot.

"ERUZIONE SCORES!" screamed Michaels from the broadcast booth. The puck was in. Team USA had the 4–3 lead. Eruzione ran on his skates, flailing his arms in the air in excitement as he celebrated the goal. All of the US players poured off the bench to mob their captain. The building erupted with cheers from the American fans.

But there were 10 minutes left to play. That was a long time against a team as talented as the Soviets. Goalie Craig, who turned down a contract with the NHL's Atlanta Flames to play in the Olympics, stood tall in net, though. He made save after save after save. Finally, the clock ticked down and Michaels delivered his famous question, "Do you believe in miracles?"

Soviet Hockey Dominance

How good were the Soviets? When people called them the best team in the world, they weren't kidding. The Soviet Union won seven of the nine Olympic gold medals between 1956 and 1988. It also won at the World Championships 14 times between 1963 and 1979. The Soviets were so good that they helped change the way the game is played. Teams had previously relied on brute force to win games. The Soviets won by using speed, skill, and precision passing. They also were the first to use a sophisticated off-ice training program.

Team USA goalie Jim Craig reacts as time winds down against Finland and the United States wins the gold medal at the 1980 Olympics.

As the American players hopped off the bench, they threw their sticks and gloves in the air. The country could feel pride thanks to 20 college kids who showed the world anything is possible. A gold medal still was not secured, though. Team USA still had to defeat Finland two days later. And team USA trailed the Finns 2–1 after two periods. It was the sixth of seven Olympic games in which Team USA trailed. But again the Americans came back. They rattled off three unanswered goals in the final 20 minutes to win 4–2. It was only the second Olympic gold medal for a US hockey team and the first since 1960.

2

Squaw Valley 1960
THE FORGOTTEN MIRACLE

The United States had always been a contender in Olympic hockey. But going into the 1960 Winter Games in Squaw Valley, California, the Americans had never won gold. They had five silver medals and one bronze medal in the first eight Olympic hockey tournaments.

Canada was the sport's first power. It won six of the first seven gold medals. Then a new dynasty began emerging in 1956. The Soviet Union, competing in its first Winter Games, took the gold. It began a streak of

US winger Weldon Olson, *left*, battles for the puck with Czechoslovakian winger Miroslav Vlach in the opening game at the 1960 Olympic Winter Games in Squaw Valley, California.

seven gold medals in nine Winter Games. The streak was interrupted in 1980 by the US Miracle on Ice Squad. Although lesser known, the 1960 US Olympic team provided the other blemish in the Soviet run.

Made in the M States

Team USA arrived in Squaw Valley with a team made up of players mostly from Minnesota and Massachusetts. Most people thought this US team would finish fourth or fifth in the 1960 tournament. Canada, Czechoslovakia, Sweden, and the Soviet Union were all thought to be better teams.

US coach Jack Riley had to make some tough decisions about his team right away. When training camp ended, Riley knew his team needed more talent. Some considered John Mayasich to be the best hockey player in the country. But he wanted to play out the season

The First Olympic Champion

Hockey first became part of the Olympics in 1920 in Antwerp, Belgium. There were no Olympic Winter Games yet. So hockey started in the Summer Games alongside sports such as swimming, gymnastics, and track and field. Canada won the first Olympic gold medal in hockey. The team was made up of players from a club in Winnipeg, Manitoba, called the Falcons. They beat the United States 2–0 in the semifinals, but a unique format allowed Team USA to still claim the silver medal. Canada allowed just one goal in the tournament.

US players, *from left*, Roger Christian, Bill Christian, and Bob McVey pose for a picture before the 1960 Winter Olympics.

with his amateur team before joining Team USA. The Minnesota legend finally joined the US squad with one practice before the Olympics. Riley also wanted to add former Harvard University star Bill Cleary. The only problem was that Bill wouldn't come unless his brother Bob would also be part of the team.

Riley agreed to bring Bob Cleary on as well. But that meant the coach had to cut three players already with the team. One of those players cut was Herb Brooks. He went on to coach the 1980 Miracle on Ice squad.

The final squad was set. Now Team USA had a tough tournament schedule to worry about. The Americans won their first four games over Czechoslovakia, Australia, Sweden, and Germany. But the upcoming medal round was going to be even tougher. They would have to play rival Canada, the Soviet Union, and Czechoslovakia again to win the gold medal. Of all the teams, the Americans most feared their northern neighbor.

"Beating the Canadians in hockey would be like Canada beating us in baseball," Bill Cleary said to the Associated Press.

Back-to-Back Silver

Team USA had never won a gold medal coming into the 1960 Winter Games. But it had come close. The Americans fell just short of gold in 1952 and 1956. The 1952 Winter Games were in Oslo, Norway. Team USA tied rival Canada but lost out on gold because of a 4–2 loss to Sweden. Four years later in Cortina d'Ampezzo, Italy, the Americans stunned the Canadians with a 4–1 win. Then they ran into the very strong Soviet team. Team USA lost 4–0 to the Soviet Union to just miss out on gold again. Team USA also won silver medals in 1920, 1924, and 1932.

Making a Run

Goalie Jack McCartan was not even expected to make the US team. He was serving in the US Army at the time. Riley asked if the military would loan the player to the Olympic team. Lucky for Team USA, the army agreed. McCartan made 39 saves in a great performance against Canada. In the second period, Paul Johnson's long slap shot on a breakaway beat the Canadian goaltender over the shoulder. The Americans earned a surprise 2–1 win.

Up next, though, the Americans had to play the defending champion Soviets. Under coach Anatoly Tarasov, the Soviet team was on its way to becoming a power. Tensions off the ice brought more attention to the game. The Cold War between the United States and the Soviet Union was starting to make Americans nervous. The home fans in Squaw Valley really wanted to see the American boys beat the Soviets. The game was an easy sellout for Blyth Arena.

The Americans scored first. That gave them a lot of confidence. But the Soviets came right back and scored a pair of goals to take a 2–1 lead. Later, American Bill Christian took a pass from brother Roger Christian. Bill ripped a shot past the Soviet goalie to tie the game midway through the second period.

The game remained tied. Time was starting to tick down. But the Christian brothers from Warroad, Minnesota, weren't done. There was a loose puck in front of the Soviet net. Bodies everywhere scrambled for the puck. Then Bill Christian shoveled the puck into the goal to give Team USA a 3–2 lead. That sent the crowd into a frenzy of cheers.

The Americans held on to win 3–2. Now they had beaten the Canadians *and* the Soviets in back-to-back games. All they had to do next was beat Czechoslovakia and the gold medal was theirs. But there was barely any time to celebrate or prepare. The final game was at eight o'clock the very next morning.

Team USA was trailing the Czechoslovakians 4–3 after two periods. The US squad gathered in the locker room to prepare for the final period. There, they got a visit from an unexpected guest. Nikolai Sologubov, the captain of the Soviet team, entered the US locker room. He wanted to share advice.

Sologubov showed the US players they could get more energy by breathing in bottled oxygen. The thin, mountain air in Squaw Valley made it harder to breathe. The bottled oxygen would help the players catch their breath. Some of the players took Sologubov's advice. It seemed to work. Team USA scored six goals in the third period. Roger Christian, who

Members of the US hockey team celebrate after beating Czechoslovakia to win the 1960 Olympic gold medal.

didn't use the oxygen machine, scored three of the goals. Team USA won the game 9–4. It won the gold medal on home ice.

Team captain Jack Kirrane accepted the gold medal on behalf of the team. After the Olympics, he returned to his job as a firefighter. Only two of the players from the 1960 US team ever made it to the NHL. They were never famous for what they did. But they will always be the first US Olympic champions in ice hockey.

3

Nagano 1998
THE NHL ARRIVES

The world's best hockey players have not always played in the Olympics. For most of the sport's history, Olympic hockey players were mostly amateurs and semi-pro players. NHL players never took part in the Winter Games.

The same situation had existed in basketball. Then the National Basketball Association (NBA) let its players go to the 1992 Olympics. The US "Dream Team" got a lot of international attention. The exposure made the NBA more popular around the world. The NHL and the

Canadian superstar Wayne Gretzky controls the puck during the 1998 Olympic Winter Games in Nagano, Japan.

International Olympic Committee (IOC) agreed that Olympic hockey should include the best players, too. So the league decided in 1995 that it would take a two-week break from its schedule. NHL players would represent their countries for the first time in the 1998 Olympic Winter Games in Nagano, Japan.

NHL commissioner Gary Bettman labeled the Olympics a "Dream Tournament." Canada, the United States, Russia, and Sweden all appeared to have very strong teams. They all had many NHL stars. Many expected them to battle for the medals. However, few people put much hope in the Czech Republic.

The Czechs had some stars of their own, though. They had Buffalo Sabres goalie Dominik Hasek. He was one of the greatest goalies in the world. They also had Jaromir Jagr. He had won two Stanley Cups with the

Unified Team Takes Gold in 1992

The early 1990s were a strange time in the world. The Soviet Union dissolved in December 1991. Many republics had made up the former Soviet Union. But they had not yet established their own Olympic teams by the Winter Games in February 1992. Instead, athletes from the former Soviet Union competed as the Unified Team. Players from today's Russia made up the majority of the hockey squad. The Unified Team remained as strong as any Soviet team of the past. It took gold with a 3–1 win over Canada. Many players on the Unified Team ended up playing in the NHL years later.

Canada's Rob Blake celebrates after scoring against Sweden during the 1998 Olympic Winter Games

Pittsburgh Penguins. The Stanley Cup is the championship trophy in the NHL. Jagr was one of the best forwards in the NHL.

It turned out that the "Dream Tournament" wasn't much of a dream for the Americans. They ended up losing to the Czech Republic 4–1 in the quarterfinals. The Czech Republic earned a date with heavily favored Canada in the semifinals. The Canadian team was filled with some of the best players in the NHL. Among them was Wayne Gretzky. He had more goals, assists, and points than anyone in NHL history. Canada also had goaltender Patrick Roy. He had already won the Stanley Cup three times.

The Czech team only had 11 players from the NHL. The rest of the team was from lower European professional leagues. The Czechs proved they could play with and beat the best when they took on the Americans. But the Canadians were a different story. Few believed the Czechs had a shot of winning.

Against All Odds

The hockey arena in Nagano was known as the Big Hat. A crowd of nearly 10,000 fans gathered there to watch the Canadians battle the Czechs. The winner would move on to the gold-medal game.

The game featured two of the best goalies in hockey history. That meant goals were hard to come by. Neither team was able to find the back of the net in the first two periods. The Czechs finally broke through in the middle of the third period. It began when the Czechs won a faceoff in Canada's zone. Defenseman Jiri Slegr took the puck on the left side of the ice near the blue line. He waited for some of the players to clear out. Then Slegr unleashed a rocket of a shot over Roy's right shoulder. Roy barely saw it. The Czech Republic now led 1–0 with 10:14 to play.

The Canadians needed a goal badly. They kept putting shots on the Czech net. But Hasek was stopping everything in sight. There was just over a minute to play when Canada finally struck.

Canadian captain Eric Lindros entered the Czech zone with speed. Hasek made two quick saves again. But after the second, the puck trickled to the side of the net. Lindros collected it and sent a hopeful pass to the front of the net. Vancouver Canucks star Trevor Linden got there at the right time. Linden lifted the puck toward the net. With Hasek on his knees, the puck found the top corner. Canada tied the game with 1:03 remaining in the third period.

That's how the period ended. And the score remained the same after a 10 minute overtime period. The game would be decided in a shootout.

Peter Forsberg's Shootout Stamp

The 1994 Winter Games in Lillehammer, Norway, were the last Olympics without NHL players. Sweden met Canada in the gold-medal game. Regulation time and overtime ended in a 2–2 tie. The game went into a shootout. That's when Sweden's seventh shooter, Peter Forsberg, scored on one of the most memorable shootout moves in history. Forsberg put the puck past Canadian goalie Corey Hirsch with just one hand on his stick. It ended up being the gold-medal winner. Forsberg's shootout move was so special that a drawing of the moment ended up on a postage stamp in Sweden.

Each team could send five players to take penalty shots to determine the winner.

Theo Fleury was the first to go for Canada. But Hasek stopped him with ease. Then Robert Reichel stepped up for the Czech Republic. He skated in on Roy with speed. Without making a move, Reichel flicked a quick shot past Roy. That gave the Czechs a 1–0 lead in the shootout.

None of the next four shooters scored. Canada's captain skated to center ice next. Lindros would have a chance to tie the Czechs. He skated in with speed and then made a nice move. Hasek sprawled to his right. Lindros let the shot go from his backhand. The puck barely nicked Hasek's stick. It fluttered in the air and clanked off the post. No goal.

Jagr had a chance to end the game for the Czechs. But his shot hit the post, too. That meant Canada's Brendan Shanahan had to score to keep the shootout going. He skated in on Hasek, made a move to his right, and tried to put the puck toward the net. Hasek was all over it and made the easy save. The Czech Republic had done the unthinkable. It beat Canada's best. Hasek's teammates mobbed him on the ice.

Two days later, Hasek was excellent again. He shut out Russia in the gold-medal game. The Czechs skated away with a 1–0 win and the country's first Olympic gold in hockey.

Goalie Dominik Hašek, *bottom left*, and his Czech Republic teammates celebrate their surprise gold medal at the 1998 Olympic Winter Games.

No one thought the Czechs could win with only 11 NHL players. They beat three of the best hockey teams in the world in the playoff round to become the first gold medalist in the NHL era of Olympic hockey.

4

Nagano 1998
THE WOMEN DEBUT

Women had been playing hockey in the United States and Canada for as long as the game had existed. But women's hockey lacked the organization and support of men's hockey. It wasn't until 1990 that women's hockey held its first World Championships. More countries began adding women's hockey during the 1990s. So the IOC decided to add the sport to the Olympic program. It debuted at the 1998 Winter Games in Nagano, Japan.

Team USA's Jennifer Schmidgall, *top*, and Canada's Therese Brisson get physical at the 1998 Olympic Winter Games in Nagano, Japan.

Team USA and Canada had developed a fierce rivalry by 1998. They were the two clear powers in women's hockey. Canada came into the Olympics as the favorite. It had won all four World Championships prior to the Nagano Games. Each time, Team USA finished second. Meanwhile, four other nations were sending women's teams to the Winter Games: China, Finland, Japan, and Sweden. But it was almost certain that the United States and Canada would meet for the gold medal.

Cammi Granato was the captain of the US squad. The Downers Grove, Illinois, native was also one of the best players in the world. On the other side, Canada had many stars of its own. Among them was goalie Manon Rheaume. She made history in 1992 when she played in an NHL preseason game with the Tampa Bay Lightning. Through 2014, she was the only woman to play in the NHL.

Game On

Both teams cruised through the preliminary round. Canada outscored its first four opponents 24–5 while Team USA had a 26–3 edge in its first four games. They finally met for the first time in the last preliminary-round game of the tournament. Both would advance to the gold-medal game regardless of the result. That didn't mean they took it easy, though.

O 1998

Team USA's Kathryn King fires a shot past Finland goalie Tuula Katriina Puputti during the preliminary round at the 1998 Olympic Winter Games.

Canada jumped out to a 4–1 lead. It looked like the Canadian dominance of women's hockey would continue. Then Team USA came alive. It scored six straight goals to shock Canada with a 7–4 win. There were more than 48 penalty minutes between the two sides in the heated game.

Each team had two days off to prepare for the first gold-medal game in the history of Olympic women's hockey. Team USA had taken first place at the end of the group stage. It went into the gold-medal game with a lot of confidence.

The gold-medal game was held in Nagano's Big Hat stadium. Nearly 9,000 screaming hockey fans showed up to watch. And like many games between the United States and Canada, the battle for the gold medal was tight from start to finish.

The first period ended with neither team scoring a goal. Canada's Rheaume and US goalie Sarah Tueting played well. Team USA seemed to be in control of the game. But the Americans couldn't put a puck past the talented Canadian goalie.

It wasn't until 2:38 into the second period that Team USA finally broke through. Gretchen Ulion, the all-time leading scorer at Dartmouth University, fired a wrist shot from the right side. The puck got past Rheaume to give the Americans a 1–0 lead. Neither team would score again in the period.

Only 20 minutes stood between Team USA and the first gold medal. Canada was not going to go quietly, though. The US squad held on to that one-goal lead with Tueting making save after save on the Canadians.

As the period neared its halfway point, the Americans went on a power play. They made it count. Sandra Whyte whizzed around the Canadian zone and fed a perfect pass to Shelley Looney. The Michigan native tapped the puck past Rheaume to make it 2–0. Even then, though, the Canadians were not to be counted out.

Danielle Goyette, whose father died the night before the Olympics opened, helped get the Canadians back in the game. Goyette was left alone in front of the US net. Hayley Wickenheiser sent a pass to the wide-open Goyette. She put it past Tueting, who barely had time to react.

Team USA had to find a way to hold off the Canadians for four more minutes to get the gold. The clock kept ticking down. Canada eventually pulled its goalie to get six skaters on the ice.

Canada Gets Its Revenge

The 2002 Olympic Winter Games were held in Salt Lake City, Utah. That meant the American women had an opportunity to win a gold medal on home ice. This time there were eight teams in the tournament. Team USA didn't meet Canada until the gold-medal game. It was worth the wait, though. Canada rode second-period goals by Hayley Wickenheiser and Jayna Hefford to a 3–2 victory. It was the country's first Olympic gold medal in women's hockey. The Americans were forced to settle for silver on home ice.

As Canada made an attempt for one more rush, Whyte jumped into the play. She picked off a Canadian pass. Whyte then skated across the red line at center ice and sent the puck toward the empty net. It crossed the goal line with eight seconds remaining in the period. Team USA was about to win gold.

As the final buzzer sounded, the American women poured off the bench. They threw their gloves into the air and piled onto each other as champions. Karyn Bye was Team USA's leading goal scorer in the tournament with five. She draped an American flag over her shoulders and skated around the ice.

"I needed that flag around me because 20 members of this team represent this country and I'm so proud to be an American," Bye told

Sweden Stuns Team USA

The 2006 Winter Olympics were in Turin, Italy. It was expected that the United States and Canada would meet once again in the gold-medal game. Sweden had other ideas. The Swedes faced the heavily favored US squad in the semifinals. After remaining tied at 2–2, the game was to be decided by a shootout. In the shootout, Sweden's Kim Martin turned aside all four American shooters she faced. Meanwhile, Maria Rooth scored twice in regulation and in the shootout to put Sweden in the gold-medal game against Canada. It was the biggest upset in women's hockey history. Sweden lost to Canada in the gold-medal game. Team USA earned the bronze over Finland.

Karyn Bye skates around the ice with the American flag after Team USA beat Canada in 1998 to win the first Olympic gold medal in women's hockey.

reporters after the game. "I don't know if it's sunk in yet, but I guess we're making history right now."

Bye was right. The American women will always be the first team to ever win Olympic gold in women's ice hockey. The US Olympic women's hockey players were the darlings of the 1998 Olympics. They even got their picture put on the Wheaties box. That showed just how much their win meant to the country and to women's hockey.

5

Salt Lake City 2002
CANADA'S TIME

There was much excitement about hockey at the 2002 Olympics. For the first time since 1980, the Winter Games were being held in the United States. Salt Lake City, Utah, was the host.

That year also marked a rather unfortunate anniversary for Canada. It had been 50 years since Canada last won an Olympic gold medal in hockey. Many Canadians were frustrated. Their country had helped invent and popularize hockey, after all. So the Canadians were on a mission.

Canada forward Paul Kariya celebrates after scoring a goal against Germany at the 2002 Olympic Winter Games in Salt Lake City, Utah.

Wayne Gretzky had failed to win a medal as a member of Canada's Olympic team in 1998. But "The Great One" was picked as the executive director for Canada's 2002 Olympic team. It was his job to find the right mix of NHL players that could finally break Canada out of its gold-medal drought.

Canada's tournament did not get off to a good start, though. Even with many of the NHL's best players, Canada lost 5–2 to Sweden in its opener. Then the Canadians barely got past Germany with a 3–2 win. A 3–3 tie with the Czech Republic followed in their third group-stage game. That meant Canada finished third in its group. It would have to play a very good Finland squad in the quarterfinals.

Gretzky was not very happy with the team's performance. He knew his team needed a boost. He also wanted to distract the media from a

Lighting the Flame

One of the great moments in any Olympic Games is when the Olympic flame is lit. That signals the beginning of the Games. The organizers of the 2002 Winter Games in Salt Lake City, Utah, wanted to make the torch lighting special. They also wanted it to be a surprise. When the torch reached the main stage, 1980 US Olympic hockey captain Mike Eruzione came out from behind the big cauldron that would house the flame. He grabbed the torch. Then he called his former teammates to the stage. Together they lit the cauldron as the crowd chanted, "USA! USA! USA!"

disappointing start to the tournament. Gretzky held a news conference after the tie with the Czech Republic. He told reporters he didn't like how the team was treated in the media and by the referees. Few people talked about the way the team played after that. Everyone talked more about Gretzky's news conference. It showed that Gretzky was willing to defend his players. It motivated the Canadian team.

Canada showed some life in the quarterfinals. It got past the Finns with a 2–1 win. That earned the team a date with Belarus in the semifinals. The Belarusians had just pulled off a huge upset over Sweden in the quarterfinals. But they were no match for Canada. The Canadians beat up on Belarus and advanced to the gold-medal game with a 7–1 win.

Belarus Stuns Sweden

The 2002 Olympic men's hockey tournament featured many exciting games. But none was as memorable as the first quarterfinal game between Belarus and Sweden. Belarus had lost all three of its preliminary-round games by a combined score of 22–6. Sweden had lost none. With less than three minutes to play, Belarus's Vladimir Kopat fired a slap shot from center ice. It bounced off Sweden goalie Tommy Salo and into the net to give Belarus a 4–3 lead. Belarus held on to win. It was one of the biggest upsets in Olympic history.

North American Showdown

If the Canadians wanted to win gold, they would have to beat the home team. The United States made the Olympic final by beating Russia 3–2 in the semifinals. The Americans were sure to have the crowd on their side. What the Americans didn't know was that the ice really belonged to Canada.

The person in charge of taking care of the ice surface at the Olympic hockey arena in Salt Lake City happened to be a Canadian. So before the tournament began, he buried a Canadian dollar coin called a Loonie at center ice.

The gold-medal game was a great one. The Americans scored first. But Canada and Team USA traded leads for much of the game. US defenseman Brian Rafalski scored a huge goal to tie the game 2–2 late in the second period. Canada's Joe Sakic of the Colorado Avalanche scored a few minutes later. The Canadians took a 3–2 lead into the final period.

The game remained close for much of the final period. The loud crowd was still cheering on their fellow Americans. Canadian goalie and New Jersey Devils legend Martin Brodeur made some outstanding saves in the third.

Canada's Paul Karlya scores against Team USA during the gold-medal game at the 2002 Olympic Winter Games.

Then Canada got a break. Sakic skated the puck up the ice with incredible speed. He then passed it off just inside the American zone to Detroit Red Wings legend Steve Yzerman. The American defenders tried to stop Yzerman. But he sent a perfect pass to Jarome Iginla. The Calgary Flames' forward was charging down the left side. Iginla ripped a heavy slap shot. US goalie Mike Richter got a piece of it. Unfortunately for the

Americans, Richter didn't get enough of it. The puck bounced off of him and trickled over the goal line.

That put Canada up 4–2. Now the Canadians just had to hold on to that lead for four more minutes. Yet not even three minutes later, Sakic broke loose again. The Canadian forward streaked down the right side of the ice. He got past the last American defenseman and put one move on Richter before putting the puck in the net. That pretty much sealed the gold medal for Canada.

For the first time since 1952, Canada was the Olympic champion in men's ice hockey. The Canadian women's hockey team also won gold that year over Team USA. Maybe that Canadian coin buried at center ice really was lucky. Dan Craig, the man who buried it, presented the "Lucky Loonie" to Gretzky after the gold-medal game. It is now in the Hockey Hall of Fame in Toronto.

6

Vancouver 2010
SID THE KID DELIVERS

Sidney Crosby broke loose from the side boards. "Iggy! Iggy!" he shouted. The NHL's biggest star was calling out to Jarome Iginla to get him the puck as he headed for the US net. It was 7:40 into overtime as Canada battled the United States in the 2010 Olympic gold-medal game.

Iginla found Crosby with a perfect pass. In one motion, Crosby flicked his wrists and glided a shot toward the US net. It looked like US goaltender Ryan Miller was in position. But as he fell to his knees to block

Canada's Sidney Crosby, *left*, and Team USA's Ryan Kesler battle for the puck during the gold-medal game at the 2010 Olympic Winter Games in Vancouver, Canada.

Sidney Crosby, *left*, celebrates after scoring to clinch the gold medal for Canada at the 2010 Olympic Winter Games.

the surprise shot from Crosby, it went under him and into the net. The nervously silent crowd exploded into a wild celebration. Canada was the king of the hockey world once again.

The 2010 Olympic Winter Games were held in Vancouver, Canada. For many Canadians, however, it might as well have been a hockey tournament. Hockey is the national sport in Canada. Plus, many agreed that Canada's 2010 Olympic team was the most talented. Fans were eager to see the Canadian team win a gold medal on home ice in the country where the sport was created.

There were some nervous moments for Canada fans in the gold-medal game. The hosts were leading 2–0 at one point. Team USA was able to get one goal back, though. And with less than a minute left in the third, Canada clung to its 2–1 lead. It was just 24.5 seconds away from winning the gold medal in regulation.

As time ticked down, young US star Patrick Kane threw a hopeful shot toward the net. The puck then glanced off the skate of US captain Jamie Langenbrunner right in front. Canada goalie Roberto Luongo made the save, but the rebound popped right onto the stick of Minnesota-born forward Zach Parise. He quickly slammed the puck into the net. The game was tied 2–2.

Team USA's MVP

The 2010 Olympic gold medal belonged to Canada. But Team USA had the Most Valuable Player of the Winter Games, Ryan Miller. He was the top goaltender in the tournament after allowing only eight goals on 147 shots against. Many considered Miller to be the real difference-maker for Team USA. He played in every game. Even in the final against Canada, he made 36 saves to keep Team USA in the game. Team USA's Brian Rafalski was named the tournament's best defenseman. Canada's Jonathan Toews earned best forward honors.

Overtime went back and forth. Both teams had some good chances to end the game. Shortly before Crosby's goal, Luongo was forced to make a big save with his shoulder on Wisconsin native Joe Pavelski. Then the Canadians went the other way to score.

The Road to Gold

The Canadians were expected to win gold in Vancouver. But they knew the Americans would be tough. Team USA had beaten Canada 5–3 when the two teams met in the preliminary round. It was a confidence-building victory for the American team. Many considered Team USA to be an underdog going into the tournament.

Instead, the roles reversed. Team USA's win over Canada meant the Americans won the group. That earned the team a bye straight into the quarterfinals. Canada would have to play an extra game in the qualification round to make it to the quarterfinals.

Many Canadians weren't feeling too good about their team after the group stage. But then Canada rolled over Germany 8–2 to earn a trip to the quarterfinals and a date with Russia. The Russians had such stars as Alex Ovechkin and Pavel Datsyuk. It wasn't going to be an easy game. But apparently someone forgot to tell Canada it wouldn't be easy.

The Canadians scored seven goals and beat the Russians with ease, 7–3. They advanced to the semifinals against Slovakia.

Slovakia had been the surprise of the tournament, and the team gave Canada a really tough game. But the Canadians won again, this time 3–2. On the other side, the Americans cruised through the playoff round. Team USA beat Switzerland 2–0 and then surprisingly dominated Finland for a 6–1 win.

The rematch between Canada and the United States was set. The Americans knew they had a chance. But Canada seemed to have destiny on its side. That proved true when it was Canada's best player ending the game with his memorable goal.

Though the Americans lost, the success of hockey at the Olympics had never been more obvious among US fans. An average of 27.6 million

Double Gold

Most of the attention was on the Canadian men's hockey team at the 2010 Winter Games. But Canada fans wanted a clean sweep of the gold medals in men's and women's hockey. Canada took on the United States in the 2010 women's final, just like the men. Canada got a pair of goals from Marie-Philip Poulin in the first period. A 28-save shutout by goalie Shannon Szabados secured the 2–0 shutout and the gold medal. Three days later, the men completed the all-Canadian sweep.

viewers watched the game on NBC. Nearly 35 million people were watching when Parise scored the game-tying goal. That made USA vs. Canada the most-watched hockey game in the United States since the 1980 Olympics. The US hockey team captured the country's attention.

"That's one of the greatest sports events I have ever seen," longtime American sports broadcaster Bob Costas said of the gold-medal game. "A script so classic that if it were a movie, they would send it back because it was unrealistic."

Over in Canada, it was estimated that nearly 80 percent of the country watched at least part of the game on TV. Hockey is the sport they love most, after all. With Crosby scoring the goal, it really was perfect. So often, he has been compared to Wayne Gretzky as one of the true greats in the game. At 22 years old, he accomplished something Gretzky never did as a player by winning the gold medal.

With Vancouver hosting the Olympics, Canadians wanted to win a lot of medals. But hockey was the most important. Anything less than gold would have marked the event as a failure. Instead, both the men's and women's teams won gold for their country. They'll all forever be heroes in Canada, but none bigger than "Sid The Kid."

7

Sochi 2014
NEXT-LEVEL RIVALS

The US Olympic women's hockey team had a 2–0 lead. It was less than four minutes away from winning gold at the 2014 Olympic Winter Games in Sochi, Russia. On the other side of the ice, however, was its oldest rival, Canada. And the three-time defending gold medalist wasn't ready to give up.

Meghan Duggan had put the US women up 1–0 midway through the second period. Then Alex Carpenter extended the lead with a power-play goal early in the third.

US players Michelle Picard (23) and Kelli Stack (16) battle with Canada's Caroline Ouellette during the 2014 Olympic gold-medal game in Sochi, Russia.

Team USA looked to be in control after that. That was until Canada's Brianne Jenner collected a puck along the boards late in the third period. She darted up the ice toward Team USA's end. She tried to cut toward the middle and threw a shot toward the net. The puck glanced off of US defenseman Kacey Bellamy and past the glove of goalie Jessie Vetter. That made it 2–1. All of the sudden, Canada had life.

Two minutes later, Canada coach Kevin Dineen pulled goalie Shannon Szabados. An extra attacker skated onto the ice. But within seconds, the decision almost was a disaster.

Canada defenseman Catherine Ward went to keep the puck inside the US zone. But a referee got in the way. The puck bounced away from Ward. It went right onto the stick of Team USA center Kelli Stack. In one motion, Stack sent the puck all the way down the ice toward the empty net. It looked to be on target. The puck wobbled closer and closer to the empty goal. Then it clanked right off the left post and stayed out of the net. That little bit of luck had kept Canada alive.

Now less than a minute remained. Canada got the puck deep into the US zone again. From the right corner, Canada forward Rebecca Johnston slid the puck toward the US net. Vetter got it with her stick, but the puck deflected right to the front. There waiting for it was Marie-Philip Poulin.

She had scored twice against Team USA in the 2010 gold-medal game. Now she calmly slid the puck from her backhand to her forehand and chipped a shot over Vetter. With 54.6 seconds remaining, the game was tied. That near miss on the post would have probably given Team USA gold. Instead, the game headed to overtime.

Heated Rivalry

The US and Canada rivalry had been heated throughout the years. The teams traded titles in the previous two World Championships, in 2012 and 2013. They also met seven times in the buildup to the Olympics. Canada won the first three. Then Team USA won the final four. The two teams met in the preliminary round in Sochi. Canada won that game 3–2.

Another Canada Gold

Canada's men and women won both hockey gold medals in 2002 and 2010. The 2014 Olympic women's gold-medal game was held on a Thursday. Canada's men attempted to do their part three days later in the men's final. After beating the US men 1–0 in the semifinals, Canada met Sweden in the final. Jonathan Toews scored in the first period. Sidney Crosby, the 2010 Olympic hero, scored once in the second period. Chris Kunitz added one more in the third. Goalie Carey Price made 24 saves for his second straight shutout in a 3–0 win. The Canadians allowed only three goals the entire Olympics en route to winning their second straight gold medal.

Canada even went through two coaches before the Olympics. Dineen took the job only two months before the Winter Games. He had a long career in the NHL but had never coached women before. Now he had his team in overtime in the gold-medal game.

The pace in overtime was fast. A penalty was called on Canada's Catherine Ward 6:09 into the extra period. That gave Team USA a power play. It was truly a golden opportunity. But it only lasted six seconds. US forward Jocelyne Lamoureux was whistled for slashing the Canadian goalie. Instead of the usual 4-on-4 in overtime, it was now 3-on-3.

Hayley Wickenheiser was Canada's second oldest player. She had played in all five Olympic women's hockey tournaments as well as the 2000 Olympic softball tournament. In overtime, Wickenheiser got the puck on a breakaway. Team USA's Hilary Knight chased her down. Knight nearly caught the Canadian. Instead, she ended up clipping Wickenheiser's heel with her own skate. Wickenheiser went down. Some thought it should have resulted in a penalty shot. Instead, the referee called a minor penalty. That meant Canada got a player back for the power play.

The Canadians made it count. With some nifty passing in the US zone, Poulin got the puck on the left side with room to shoot. She didn't miss. Poulin put home her second goal to give Canada another gold.

A US player skates off the ice as the Canadian players celebrate their gold-medal victory in overtime at the 2014 Olympic Winter Games.

For the Americans, it couldn't have been a more heartbreaking defeat. They led 2–0 with less than four minutes to play. To come that close and end up with silver for the second time in four years was very difficult. For the Canadians, it was another gold medal to add to the three won previously.

"It's an amazing feeling to win the way we did," Jenner said after the game. "It just shows our character. We believed the whole time."

The 2014 gold-medal game may end up being remembered as one of the greatest hockey games ever played at the Olympics, men's or women's.

Great
Olympians

Jim Craig (USA)
Team USA's goalie stopped 92 percent of the shots he faced in the 1980 Olympics en route to a gold medal.

Sidney Crosby (Canada)
Crosby scored the game-winning goal for Canada on home ice at the 2010 Olympics and helped Canada win another gold in 2014.

Peter Forsberg (Sweden)
Forsberg scored the game-winning goal in a shootout against Canada in the gold-medal game at the 1994 Olympics. He represented Sweden at four Olympics, winning gold in 2006 as well.

Cammi Granato (USA)
Granato captained Team USA to the first gold medal awarded in women's hockey at the 1998 Olympics. She also was Team USA's leading scorer at the 2002 Olympics, where Team USA took silver.

Dominik Hasek (Czech Republic)
In 1998, the Czech goalie led his team to a surprise gold medal in one of his four Olympics.

Jack McCartan (USA)
His 39-save performance against Canada in the 1960 medal round might be the greatest performance ever by a US goalie.

Teemu Selanne (Finland)
Selanne is one of only two men to have appeared in six Olympics in hockey. He won one silver medal and three bronzes.

Vladislav Tretiak (Soviet Union)
With three gold medals and one silver, he is the most decorated goalie in Olympic hockey history.

Hayley Wickenheiser (Canada)
The five-time Olympian has four gold medals and one silver. She was also a 2000 Olympian in softball.

Glossary

AMATEUR
An athlete who cannot receive money for competing.

BLUE LINES
The two lines that divide an ice hockey rink into three equal zones: the offensive zone, neutral zone, and defensive zone.

COMMISSIONER
The chief executive of a sports league.

DYNASTY
A team that wins multiple championships in a short period of time.

PENALTY SHOT
An unhindered shot at the goal awarded to a player if an opponent denies a scoring opportunity by taking a penalty. Penalty shots are also used as part of a shootout.

POWER PLAY
When an opposing player commits a penalty and his or her team has to play down a player until the penalty expires.

RED LINE
The line on a hockey rink that divides the ice in half.

RIVALRY
Intense competitiveness between players or teams.

SHOOTOUT
A shooting competition that is used to determine the winner of a game if it is tied after regulation and overtime.

SLAP SHOT
A shot in hockey that involves swinging at and slapping the puck with great force.

WRIST SHOT
A quick shot in hockey that is made when a player sweeps the puck forward and snaps his or her wrists to lift the puck.

For More
Information

SELECTED BIBLIOGRAPHY

Forgotten Miracle. Dirs. Tommy Haines and Andrew Sherburne. Golden Puck Pictures, 2009. DVD.

Podnieks, Andrew. *Canadian Gold: 2010 Olympic Winter Games Ice Hockey Champions*. Plattsburgh, NY: Fenn Publishing, 2010.

Thompson, Harry. "Revenge was a dish best served gold." *USA Hockey 75th Anniversary Commemorative Program*. 2012. 42–43.

Wallechinsky, David, and Jaime Loucky. *The Complete Book of the Winter Olympics: 2010 Edition*. London, UK: Aurum Press 2009.

FURTHER READINGS

Allen, Kevin. *Star-Spangled Hockey: Celebrating 75 Years of USA Hockey*. Chicago, IL: Triumph, 2011.

Coffey, Wayne. *The Boys of Winter: The Untold Story of a Coach, a Dream, and the 1980 US Olympic Hockey Team*. New York: Three Rivers Press, 2005.

Podnieks, Andrew. *Where Countries Come to Play: Celebrating the World of Olympic Hockey and the Triple Gold Club*. Plattsburgh, NY: Fenn-M&S, 2013.

Zweig, Eric. *Long Shot: How the Winnipeg Falcons Won the First Olympic Hockey Gold*. Toronto, ON: Lorimer, 2007.

WEBSITES

To learn more about Great Moments in Olympic Sports, visit **booklinks.abdopublishing.com**. These links are routinely monitored and updated to provide the most current information available.

PLACES TO VISIT

Hockey Hall of Fame
Brookfield Place
30 Yonge Street
Toronto, Ontario M5E 1X8
(416) 360-7765
www.hhof.com
The Hockey Hall of Fame is full of hockey history. Its World of Hockey exhibit is one of its largest. There are many items from past Olympics. The World of Hockey exhibit is also home to the International Ice Hockey Federation Hall of Fame, which includes many great Olympians.

Olympic Center – 1980 Rink Herb Brooks Arena
2634 Main St.
Lake Placid, NY 12946
(518) 523-1655
www.whiteface.com/facilities/olympic-center
The site of the 1980 Olympic hockey tournament and the Miracle on Ice has been well preserved. Fans can take guided tours and even go for a skate on the same ice where Team USA beat the Soviets. There's also an Olympic Museum inside with exhibits from both the 1980 and 1932 Olympic Winter Games, which Lake Placid also hosted.

Index

Belarus (men), 41

Brooks, Herb (coach), 8–9, 18

Bye, Karyn, 36–37

Canada (men), 4, 15, 16, 18,
19, 20, 24, 25–28, 39–44,
47–52, 57

Canada (women), 31–36, 51,
52, 55–59

Christian, Bill, 19–20

Christian, Roger, 19–21

Cleary, Bill, 17–18

Craig, Jim, 8, 11, 12

Crosby, Sidney, 47–48, 50, 52, 57

Czech Republic (men), 24–29,
40, 41

Czechoslovakia (men), 9, 16,
18, 20

Eruzione, Mike, 8, 11–12, 40

Finland (men), 9, 13, 40, 41, 51

Finland (women), 32, 36

Forsberg, Peter, 27

Germany (men), 18, 40, 50

Gretzky, Wayne, 25, 40–41, 44, 52

Hasek, Dominik, 24, 27–28

Jagr, Jaromir, 24–25, 28

Jenner, Brianne, 56, 59

Johnson, Mark, 10–11

Mayasich, John, 16–17

Miller, Ryan, 47, 49

Myshkin, Vladimir, 11, 12

Parise, Zach, 49, 52

Poulin, Marie-Philip, 51, 56–57,
58

Rheaume, Manon, 32, 34–35

Roy, Patrick, 26, 28

Russia (men), 24, 28, 42, 50–51

Sakic, Joe, 42, 43, 44

Schneider, Buzz, 9–10

Slovakia (men), 51

Soviet Union (men), 7–12, 15,
16, 18, 19–20

Sweden (men), 8, 9, 16, 18, 24,
27, 40, 41, 57

Sweden (women), 32, 36

Szabados, Shannon, 51, 56

Tueting, Sarah, 34–35

Unified Team (men), 5, 24

United States (men)
1920, 4, 16, 18
1924, 18
1932, 18
1952, 18
1956, 18
1960, 13, 15–21
1980, 7–13, 16, 18, 40
1998, 24 , 25
2002, 42–44
2010, 47–52
2014, 57

United States (women)
1998, 31–37
2002, 35, 44
2006, 36
2010, 51
2014, 55–59

Whyte, Sandra, 35, 36

Wickenheiser, Hayley, 35, 58

ABOUT THE AUTHOR

Chris Peters is a writer based in North Liberty, Iowa. He is a contributor to CBSSports.com and *USA Hockey Magazine* and is the editor of UnitedStatesofHockey.com. The Chicago native has written children's books on the Stanley Cup Finals and girls' hockey. Peters served three years as a public relations coordinator for USA Hockey. He resides with his wife and son.